Metrognomic Tales

Also by Betty McKenzie-Tubb and published by Ginninderra Press

Wordfall

Meanderings

Betty McKenzie-Tubb

Metrognomic Tales

Thanks

My grateful thanks to Sandra Seth and Jen Gibson who helped this Luddite with their time and technical skills. Thanks also to my writing friends who listened to my tales and, of course, to Ginninderra Press for agreeing to publish them.

Metrognomic Tales
ISBN 978 1 76109 023 3
Copyright © Betty McKenzie-Tubb 2020

First published 2020 by
GINNINDERRA PRESS
PO Box 3461 Port Adelaide 5015
www.ginninderrapress.com.au

Contents

Prologue	7
Metrognomic Tales – The First: 2006	9
'This Solitude Covered with Iron…': 2006	11
The Joys of the Omnibus: 2006	14
Opposite: 2007	16
A Metrognomic Tale in Autumn: 2012	18
Loss: 2013	20
The Cat Lady: 2013	22
Two Men: 2013	24
Deep Purple: 2014	26
Mystery Man: 2014	28
The Girl with the Dragonfly Tattoo: 2014	30
The Cat Lady – another encounter: 2014	32
Commuting in Company: 2016	34
A Reduced Circle: 2017	36
A Ballet of Fingers: 2017	38
The Handkerchief: 2018	40
A Statement of Fact: 2019	43
A Digital Misadventure: 2019	45
Finis: 2019	46
A Disrupted Journey – a tale told in dreadful doggerel	48

Prologue

There won't be many of you who would have been at high school in the 1940s.

I was. Studying English, as we all did, there were certain texts which stand out in my memory.

There were the usual plays of Shakespeare – beginning, of course, with *A Midsummer Night's Dream*, deemed suitable for twelve- and thirteen-year-olds, then moving on to dark *Julius Caesar*, *Hamlet* and *Macbeth*. We studied the essays of writers like Chesterton, Lamb, and Hazlitt; the short stories of H.G. Wells, Wilkie Collins et al.

A particular story by E.M. Forster stayed in my memory. It was titled 'The Celestial Omnibus'. I couldn't remember the details so I recently purchased – for the princely sum of five dollars – *The Celestial Omnibus and Other Tales*.

A boy comes upon the Celestial Omnibus by lucky chance and takes two journeys, with a different driver each time. The first, the wordy Sir Thomas Browne, the second Dante Alighieri of frightening aspect. On the second journey, the boy is accompanied by Mr Bons – read backwards – a pompous haughty gentleman, president of the local Literary Society and the proud owner of *seven* volumes of Shelley.

The omnibus was travelling to a heaven occupied by characters from literature and myth. Fresh eyed and honest, admiring Mrs Gamp and Mrs Harris as well as Achilles and Wagner, the boy was lauded there. The pretentious Mr Bons, despite his knowledge of the giants of literature, was hurled into what the reader supposes was Dante's inferno.

My bus journeys have never terminated in a celestial city, though Hobart is pretty close to being one, nor do the following tales make reference to writing luminaries.

Metrognomic Tales – The First: 2006

As my title suggests, I am a person of short stature and this presents some difficulties when travelling by bus, which I have done regularly since my husband died. My legs are too short to enable me to brace myself against the face of the facing seat as the bus driver navigates the many and sudden curves which characterise my particular route into town. I either cling desperately to the arm rail or hope that the person who chooses to sit next to me will be large so that I will be wedged and no movement of any kind is possible. I also have to ignore the convenient single front seat. The step up to it is too high and I struggle to descend with dignity.

If I board a so-called 'kneeling bus', my egress is smooth because the vehicle becomes level with the kerb, but if not, I have to execute a flying leap onto terra firma. Dignity and knees suffer terribly.

However, with an attempt at the cadence of Shakespeare, I come not to denigrate travel by bus, but to praise it.

I know that I am often pitied by friends, neighbours and members of my family for lacking car ownership and, I suppose, a certain status that goes with it but, in fact, I have some pity for those whose car is like a third limb, the amputation of which would be painful indeed. For some, it is a necessity, but for many to drive is a habit and they miss so much engagement with their fellows.

So many interesting people use public transport and I have been privileged to meet some of them. In some cases, I have heard their personal stories; in others, I have to surmise, and that exercises the imagination. Let me tell you about one of these people.

He is a middle-aged man and I know him to be unemployed and poor. His clothes are cheap but scrupulously clean, as are his runners.

His hair is longish and he wears a beanie, so I suppose he fits the description sometimes used when speaking of bogans.

Until recently, we have exchanged greetings when we meet at the bus shelter and have engaged in phatic conversation about the weather and so on. However, I'd noticed that he'd often looked downcast and one day I overheard scraps of his conversation with a gentleman who seemed to know him. He was speaking about things 'not looking good' and 'perhaps needing surgery'.

Our greetings have extended into conversations and not long ago he extended his hand and said, 'I'm Brian' (not his real name) 'by the way.'

I shook his hand and replied, 'I'm Betty,' believing that one gains or loses respect by actions and not by titles.

Brian is well spoken and, I suspect, an autodidact. It seems that whatever subject arises, he knows something about it. When I told him that I'd been to the Vienna exhibition recently held in Melbourne and the simplicity of some of the furniture, he went on to talk about Shaker furniture and from there to Quakerism and the existence of God, neither of us knowing anything about the latter.

Brian is a sandy man. His hair is reddish and his skin shows the ravages of overexposure to the sun. There are some small scars which may be the result of biopsies or excisions, so I was not entirely surprised that he had a brain tumour. He was, at the time of this revelation, having chemotherapy. No wonder he often looked dispirited!

However, a day or so ago when we met at the bus shelter, he was looking very cheerful indeed.

'Have I told you,' he asked, 'that I've been to see my oncologist and there is absolutely no sign of my tumour? He says that I'm not cured but that I'm certainly in remission.' He expressed it in algebraic terms: CX, MX=R. No cancer, no metastasis, equals remission.

'If I had a bottle of champers, I'd open it at once,' I said, and we clicked imaginary glasses.

How could I have witnessed such joy or had such a happy tale to tell if I'd been insulated from the world in a little sardine tin on wheels?

'This Solitude Covered with Iron…': 2006

('Driving Towards the Lac Qui Parle River' – Robert Bly)

Passionados, petrol-heads, speed merchants, social climbers will certainly not agree with me when I state that the motor car has much to answer for. There are, of course, those for whom it's a necessity, but I'm focusing on the negatives.

Apart from the noise, pollution, bullying and pedestrian hazard caused by this means of travel, there is an equally serious implication, as I have already indicated: its socially cocooning effect. Motorists miss out on an amazing number of slices of life.

Of course there has to be a certain amount of subjectivity in what I have to say because I am a regular bus traveller and at the moment (since my legs are still functional) glad to be such. I'm able to observe my fellow passengers and at times engage in conversation with them. I'm aware that some are unused to public transport and don't know that they must validate their tickets or how to do so. Despite the arrow which suggests the direction in which the ticket should be inserted in the machine, they place it back to front and to their bewilderment and embarrassment it is spat out. This sometimes happens two or three times before the driver recommends, somewhat testily, that arrowhead first would be a good idea.

Occasionally – very occasionally – an elegantly clad and coifed lady climbs into the bus and, looking neither right nor left, selects her seat and sits as if she has graced the passengers with her presence, and she somehow suggests she is certainly not in the habit of using this mode of travel. Strangely enough, when a certain immaculately attired gentleman makes a rare appearance, he does scan the passengers and smile or even greet them verbally. It seems that snobbery is chiefly the domain of women and I wonder why this is so. It would be a good subject for a PhD.

On gaining her licence, a young woman of my acquaintance exclaimed with glee, 'I'll never have to travel by bus again! Only the poor and elderly do that.' Well, there's some truth in her observation, though I've yet to discover that either poverty or old age are sins.

Last week, I witnessed two incidents outside the norm.

I had a window seat and next to me was a rather large, youngish woman. Across the aisle was a big man with a very deep depression in his forehead, the result, I supposed, of some accident or perhaps surgery. Accompanying him was an elderly little person who seemed to be his mother as she held his hand in that peculiarly maternal way.

I was gazing through the window observing autumn gardens, when I became aware of movement beside me and saw that my travelling companion was leaning across the aisle and supporting the large man in his seat. I could see his legs shaking violently; his head was thrown back and his whole body convulsed.

'Has anyone a mobile phone?' the supporter asked in a loud voice.

The driver heard, observed the situation in his mirror, stopped the bus and phoned for an ambulance. Meanwhile, the poor man continued to shake for some time and his little companion mutely held his hand.

We waited for half an hour before the ambulance arrived and the paramedics took charge. Meantime, the victim's spasms had ceased but he was dazed and barely coherent when questioned. It was thought that he could walk off the bus, as he'd walked on, but he had become paralysed on his right side and had to be strapped into a chair and wheeled to the waiting stretcher.

I had observed kindness and resourcefulness and, amongst the passengers, patience and calm. In a car, I might have seen the ambulance whizzing by and have wondered very briefly about the person within.

The very next day, I was travelling home from town, again using the window seat at right angles to the space for wheelchairs and pushers, when a young mother with a toddler in a stroller entered the bus.

Sitting next to me was a big middle-aged man who'd boarded in the city and had immediately immersed himself in a book. Casually I looked across hoping to see what he was reading with such rapt attention. I noticed that he'd reached page five but couldn't, without glasses, see the text.

When the young woman placed the pusher in the designated space, there was no room for her to sit, so she hung on to the pusher with one hand and clung to the railing of the luggage rack with the other. My travelling companion didn't look up – indeed, hadn't raised his eyes from his book once since boarding, and my glare had no effect upon him whatsoever.

A gentleman of middle-eastern appearance sitting opposite the mother offered her his seat but she refused because she couldn't relinquish her hold on the pushchair. I didn't think she would accept the seat of an elderly woman, so didn't offer.

Eventually, she and the child left the bus and still the big man read on. After some time, I glanced again at the book. He was still intently reading page five! He got off at my stop, as it happened, and there was something about his demeanour which suggested that all was not well with him.

The disgust which I'd felt at his seeming utter boorishness diminished and was replaced by pity. Things are not always what they seem, and this particular truth was emphasised on this journey.

What does a motorist learn on any given day? That other 'bloody drivers' should not be on the road?

The Joys of the Omnibus: 2006

On the way to the bus the other day, I encountered a neighbour, Sue. The conversation went something like this.
Me: 'Hello, Sue.'
Sue (eyeing my shopping bag): 'Where are you off to?'
Me: 'To the shops. I need a few groceries.'
Sue: 'Oh, you poor thing. You have to use the bus.'

I didn't feel the need to be pitied even though, when I embark on these errands, I frequently buy more than what is on my list. The bag which I have to lug home is often uncomfortably heavy. However, as always, I am compensated by a journey which affords me pleasure.

I have gained bus friends. The bus shelter is our common ground and we don't often meet anywhere else unless by accident in some coffee shop, like the popular local café.

Not all the people who gather at my stop could be called friends but they are close acquaintances and we have been meeting there for years. Most have led very interesting lives, I slowly discover, and would inhabit a novel very well.

There is the Exercise Man, who seemingly has a psychiatric problem or is perhaps over-medicated. He cannot stay still; he flexes his muscles, performs leg exercises. Once in the bus, he wriggles his fingers and massages his scalp, his face, neck and arms.

Then there is the Asian Lady who joins our motley crew a little further on. She wears flowers or ribbons in her hair, sings softly to herself. She seems happy and is not disturbed by the stares of other passengers.

There are three siblings, two young women and their brother. I know they are siblings because they so strongly resemble each other, and board and alight at the same point. They resemble each other in their chinlessness. They do not usually sit together. The young man is dressed like a public servan:; dark suit, shirt and tie, black shoes instead of the ubiquitous dirty runners.

The sisters dress differently. The overweight one with the intelligent face wears her thick dark hair in a braid; her clothes may have been pre-loved. The younger one, who alights at the university, sports the garb currently in vogue amongst the young: short skirt, patterned stockings, boots. Apart from the unfortunate meagre chin, she is very pretty and has well cut thick hair.

There is one person I'm always delighted to meet. Like me, she is elderly and widowed. Unlike me, she used to be a car driver but now uses public transport. She is always elegantly attired and, though very frail in appearance, has great zest for living and has recently been to China. She plans to visit New Delhi soon, where her son has been posted. Coincidentally, my granddaughter's husband has also been posted there and I should like to visit the family. Perhaps this fellow traveller will also be my plane companion.

Opposite: 2007

Opposite…what an evocative word! It's redolent of politics, religion, societies, of men from Mars and women from Venus, of dichotomies within one's own self. Disregarding these larger issues, let me regale you (or so I hope) with the details of a recent encounter with an opposite.

In the bus the other day, I sat (as it happened) opposite a group of young people who were, I gathered from their less than muted conversation, university students.

The boys were rather pimply and gauche, as many boys of that age are wont to be.

The only girl among them was quite the opposite. She had perfect skin, albeit heavily made-up, and she was pretty with that prettiness which ages well; not with that chocolate box prettiness which tends to become amorphous, but with features which, enlarged in old age, would be considered distinguished. Somewhat overweight, she sat like a man, knees apart, her short, frilly, bright pink skirt only just allowing some decorum.

What does this have to do with opposite? Well, there I sat – small, dumpy, ageing, dressed, as it happened, entirely in black – and there she sat, absolutely the blonde Goddess of Bling! There were sparkles in her hair and from her ears hung rhinestone earrings like miniature chandeliers, Her low-cut, skimpy top sported a glittering brooch pointed like an arrow at her ample cleavage and the denim jacket worn over it had multiple badges on the lapels. Without the benefit of glasses, I couldn't see the messages the badges conveyed. But perhaps that was just as well. There were glittering bracelets on her wrists and rings on every finger; her nails, in contrast, painted black. Of course she wore trainers – what self-respecting teenager wouldn't – but the laces were multicoloured with bejewelled aglets.

The wonder of all this is that there wasn't a hint of tartiness. Her direct, clear gaze and her pleasant, if rather loud voice, her supreme self-confidence, indicated that there would be, sometime in the future, a dramatic change and the confident girl would morph into a poised adult sure of her place in the world and probably with a carapace of conservatism.

She impressed me but I'm sure that I, her opposite, who wonders, as life travels nearer its end, what has it all been about, warranted no more than a fleeting glance and it's doubtful whether the Goddess of Bling is sitting at her desk recording impressions of me.

A Metrognomic Tale in Autumn: 2012

It is that serene and lovely season, autumn, and I should be writing about it. However, it has been done many times before and better than I ever could. Who could hope to match Keats' 'season of mist and mellow fruitfulness' or Shakespeare's dark metaphor for unhappy ageing: '…my way of life / is fall'n into the sere, the yellow leaf'?

This morning as I sat in the bus shelter in the gentle autumn sun, my bus friend, Brian, whom I had not seen for some time, joined me.

The last time we conversed he had been told by his oncologist that his cancer was in remission. We raised our imaginary champagne flutes and drank a toast to that.

I learnt this morning that his cancer had returned and in full force. He acknowledged with his usual courage and lack of self-pity that his life would not be greatly prolonged despite aggressive treatment with radiation and chemotherapy.

He changed the subject of his illness, noticing that I held in my hand T.S. Eliot's *Four Quartets*. He admitted that he did not know Eliot and favoured the poetry of the beat generation, naming Jack Kerouac and Allen Ginsberg. I confessed that I had heard of those writers but was not really familiar with their works. Touché!

I am regularly astonished at the wide range of Brian's knowledge, but why should I be? There are many autodidacts who often display more knowledge and understanding than an equal number of university graduates, especially these days when degrees are valued mostly for their utility.

Brian is no longer in the workforce and I do not know what his employment was. He is from Western Australia and has the ravaged complexion which constant exposure to the sun bestows upon sandy-haired Celts. I do not ask questions. This reticence is not due to lack of curiosity but because I do not want to appear nosey. Sometimes long acquaintance can lead to voluntary revelations.

Brian is not a Roman Catholic but I believe he attended a Roman Catholic school. The brothers, especially the Jesuits, can be good educators in the strictly academic sense. Maybe they inculcated in my bus friend a love of learning.

It is with sadness that I reflect that I may not be able to enjoy these interesting chats with Brian for much longer. Already he is having the attention of a palliative care team. He is still having treatment despite its futility.

I raise my own imaginary glass again to toast a brave man who, in the autumn of his life, has no illusions.

Loss: 2013

I haven't added to my store of metrognomic tales lately but in the last week or so I have been very aware of some of my bus friends – or rather, their absence.

The last time I spoke to Brian, he looked and sounded very ill indeed and I suspected he had not much longer to live. For the first time in our long acquaintance, he was not his stoic self and complained of his suffering. This was hardly surprising and I continue to be amazed at what was, in the past, his cheerfulness in the face of imminent death, his interest in world affairs and his concern for the welfare of others.

Last week, I caught up with the Cat Lady (of whom, more later) and she informed me that Brian had died. If I had taken *The Mercury* daily, I would have known, since I knew his surname, and I regret I was not one of the locals who bade him goodbye. I think there would not have been many.

Brian lived in one of the villas belonging to the housing department. The residents in these villas all seem to be people who have known better times and I feel they have interesting life stories. They seem to have formed a close-knit little community whose members look out for each other. I wish I knew Brian's story but there is a fine line between genuine interest and prying and I am reluctant to cross it. However, I shall remember him as a courteous, compassionate and articulate man and perhaps that is knowledge enough. I heard that his funeral was a Buddhist affair and in his will he directed that those who attended go to the small local café and bakery, and have a coffee at his expense. How completely in character that was.

The Cat Lady was one whom I had not seen for some time. This recent encounter was a great shock. One eye was hideously red and swollen and there was a great wad of sticking plaster down the length of her nose and across the bridge above the nostrils. I was aghast and thought she must have been involved in some terrible accident.

No. She said she had been concerned about a very small lump on the side of her nose. Her doctor thought it should be investigated and it was found to be cancerous. The later large excision was closed with fifty stitches. She lives alone but was sent home afterwards even though she had a general anaesthetic.

Fortunately, a kind neighbour permitted her to stay overnight in his villa, surrendering his bed. He slept on his couch and checked on her regularly.

The Cat Lady, back in her own villa, soon after, found herself on the floor, having had, she supposed, a seizure like the ones she had before her brain surgery.

Our bus is a sad one at the moment. I keep my eye on the troubled Exercise Man and was more than glad to meet my friend 'P', whose son is with the United Nations Organisation and posted in New Delhi, where my granddaughter and family are, so we exchange news.

She is a frail little lady whose health is not good and I had intended to ring her so am glad that she is in every sense 'on board'.

What I am waiting for at the moment is the appearance of the youngish woman whose name I consistently forget but whose pretty face, ready smile and cheerful conversation lighten the day. She is a nurse, now in administration, and I think that a pity, since I feel sure her patients must have mistaken her for a ministering angel and felt the better for it. When she reappears, I certainly shall.

The Cat Lady: 2013

There has been an increase in kindness and deference towards me lately and, instead of wondering why, I realise I am seen as being old. Me? At eighty-five? Surely not.

It has been a while since I have met the Cat Lady at the bus stop but the other day there she was; rough-hewn and cheerful as ever. The nose which had been slit to remove a tumour had healed wonderfully and of course her eye is no longer bruised and swollen.

She greeted me cheerfully and, when the bus arrived, guided me into it solicitously. We sat together and, as we travelled, she opened the large album she was clutching and showed me photographs of her three cats. I am rather fond of cats and the images were clear and sometimes amusing, but after the first twenty or so, the viewing became somewhat tedious.

Arriving at our destination, she alighted first and held out her hand to steady me as I followed her. For this, I was actually grateful. If the bus is not a so-called 'kneeling bus' (and this one was not), the jump down jars my knees and I invariably mutter 'ouch'.

We walked a short way together. When we reached the ATM, I told her I was going to withdraw some money We said goodbye and I carried out my transaction. Turning to continue walking, I spotted the Cat Lady hovering a few metres away.

'I just wanted to see that you were OK,' she explained, thinking I could be open to attack and robbery.

I thanked her and farewelled her for a second time. She was going to forge ahead but I needed to cross the road and told her so.

'Would you like me to help you across?' she asked.

My response was indignation, which I concealed. Who could be angry at such concern? 'No, thank you,' I replied, 'I'm quite OK,' and walked away with as brisk a step as I could summon.

Life throws up little ironies. I heard later that on that very day, the Cat Lady somehow tripped and fell in the middle of Sandy Bay Road. She was shaken but not hurt, very fortunate not to have been run over by a car on what is a very busy thoroughfare.

I shall miss the Cat Lady when she eventually transfers to a housing development unit on the north-west coast, her home place. She has a heart of gold and I am grateful for what is, at present, her needless solicitude.

Two Men: 2013

One person whom I have not mentioned recently is the Exercise Man. He continues to be quite unable to stand or sit still. His movements are unusual, not to say bizarre.

At our bus stop, he performs those leg stretching exercises using the nearby telegraph pole as a brace. There are names for these activities but being a person of the non-sporting variety I do not possess the nomenclature to describe them.

On boarding the bus and seating himself in the one-person-only front seat, he begins his massage: first his scalp, then his jaw, then neck, then arms. He flexes his fingers, runs them through his mop of thick, dark, curly hair. These actions are repetitive.

It has taken us both a long time to engage in conversation. It began when he actually sat down beside me as we waited in the shelter one morning. He unexpectedly expressed admiration for the jacket I was wearing. I was surprised and rather chuffed not to be the often invisible old woman.

He is himself clinically clean and dresses as well as his straitened circumstances allow. He has previously referred to his poverty and lives in public housing.

I had suspected that he was what we no longer call a New Australian. Because he has a swarthy complexion, I hazarded a guess (in retrospect, a wild one) that he was from the Mediterranean. His accent is rather thick but his English vocabulary excellent. As time went by, we discussed all manner of things. While he is talking, his compulsive movements stop.

He is, in fact, from one of those exotic countries in the Balkans; well educated, a professional of some kind, but I have not yet discovered

– as I am loath to ask directly – why he left his country. There are intimations that it was for political reasons, perhaps related to Soviet communism. He said that he learnt Russian at school and has spoken about communism, which, he says, seems bland and innocuous but which has a dark underbelly of spying and informing.

There has been a suggestion that his father was a victim of the regime but this is only my surmise. As I recently reacquainted myself with *Northanger Abbey*, I know that false assumptions arising from a fevered imagination are best avoided.

I ask the Exercise Man about the economy of his small country. He tells me that it is frail with little industries beginning but failing because of lack of finance. He confessed that, though he rings his mother frequently, he is rather out of touch with the economy of his homeland and has to gain information via his computer.

We spoke about Italy and its hilarious politics and one day rejected the idea that Berlusconi would ever regain power.

The next week he said, 'By the way, we were wrong about Berlusconi.'

But I am afraid I had lost track of Italian politics and did not know who the leader was. I guessed he would be temporary, anyway.

I continued to wonder why, when the Exercise Man sits alone in the bus, he continues to engage in these strange massaging movements. Cathy Morland's fevered imagination comes into play again. I wonder whether he was tortured,; perhaps confined, so that he was not permitted to exercise outdoors. This is a mystery that I should like unravelled.

In the meantime, I rejoice in being a bus traveller because my life is thus enriched.

Deep Purple: 2014

My theory about people who wear purple is no secret to my long suffering friends; I repeat it ad nauseam. It is my belief that these lovers of purple are either creative or mad. I have no scientific evidence to back me; I am an empiricist and rely on observation.

Today I travelled by bus, as is my wont. Waiting for my conveyance, I sat on the provided bench and beside me was a woman wearing a rather beautiful jacket in – you guessed it – purple. I could not resist telling her how lovely it was. She confessed that purple was her favourite colour. It must have been quite obvious to her that I was of like mind since I was wearing a lavender pullover and purple corduroy jacket; my legs were encased in tights of a similar colour and my shoes, ditto. I dared to ask her (because I am desperate to collect data which will support my theory) whether she painted or wrote or engaged in any other creative activity. Unfortunately, she shook her head.

Only recently, I have been searching for a photograph of me at nineteen, wearing a purple dress made by the wonderful aunt whose talent with the needle was phenomenal. She used a Vogue pattern, rather unusually, because she was quite able to conjure up a garment using only the prospective recipient's sketch as a guide. The photograph was taken by one of the ubiquitous street photographers who made their appearance on the Sydney streets at that time. This was 1947.

I was wearing the aforementioned dress; in addition, a white beret, white suede gloves, purple stockings and black ankle-strap shoes. I carried a black drum-shaped handbag. At nineteen, one's face, be it plain or pretty, is anyway at its best. I was happy, I was tops, I felt great and *I want that photo*, if only to prove to my grandchildren that I was once young. A photo is needed as I recall the words of H.G. Wells when he describes a character in one of his tales – 'Wrinkled and [withered] with age [you] could not fix it or fill it with youth'.

My bus arrived and I climbed aboard and found my seat. Shortly after, a woman sat down beside me and what was she wearing? Purple! I refrained from questioning her about her creativity or lack of it. If she had replied in the negative, it would have been a blow too many.

We joked about the colour in question and when the 'Next stop' sign appeared, we laughed. It boasted a purple background.

Mystery Man: 2014

'Another beautiful day in paradise,' said one of my fellow bus travellers who sat across the aisle from me. Of course I agreed. This was the third day of unremitting sunshine and it is still winter.

I like this fellow traveller. I am ashamed to admit that my first encounter with him did not give me a favourable impression. He was not dirty but unkempt, with crumpled clothes and a warm woollen Scandinavian bonnet. His nose was swollen and almost purple, the nose of an alcoholic, his cheeks red-veined. Not entirely unexpectedly, he reeked of whisky.

I have met him often since. Our quiet conversation took place when we shared a seat at the bus stop. Something triggered our exchange of views about our present federal government and we found we were of like mind. He is well spoken, and, I discovered, university educated. He admitted somewhat ruefully that he had been a contemporary of a well known federal politician when a student at UTAS.

It is my custom to give names to the people in my *Metrognomic Tales* and I find myself in a dilemma about the christening of this gentleman (for gentleman he is). Perhaps I shall refer to him as the Mystery Man, for I wonder what has reduced him to his present state. He seems to fill himself with alcohol every day. Although he never staggers or stumbles, his face is aflame, his eyes watery. If a match came in contact with his breath, it would surely ignite.

How has it come to this? Has he a wife or children? I think not, but this is mere speculation. He has seen much better days and even now alights from the bus and walks down a street of expensive houses on the waterside.

I wonder whether he sometimes looks at the mountain and says to himself, as I do, 'I will lift up mine eyes unto the hills whence cometh my help.' Perhaps not.

Whatever misfortune has caused his present condition, I am glad that he still thinks, with me, that he lives in paradise.

The Girl with the Dragonfly Tattoo: 2014

Travelling by bus enriches my life in some small way: I love watching the young, most deeply in love with their mobile phones, the ageing women fresh from their Friday appointments with their hairdresser, the Asian students, the young mothers with their children, the wearers of purple who, I'm sure, are engaged in some creative process.

A few passengers have about them an aura of mystery and such was the tall girl who was standing (all seats were occupied) near me. I was fortunately seated and in a position to observe.

Those of you who have read Stieg Larsson's *The Girl with the Dragon Tattoo* will be familiar with Lisbeth's mode of dressing, her piercings and the dragon tattoo on her shoulder. You would see the resemblance between her and the young woman who recently boarded the bus at Franklin Square and alighted at Red Chapel Avenue in Sandy Bay. She was quite beautiful, sporting what was obviously an expensive haircut. Her skin was enviably flawless. She carried herself proudly; the garment she wore flowed. It was not of the kind which can be bought at an Indian-style shop but was so composed that it might have been a model. It was Nile green with a scooped-out back. Surely an admirer of Lisbeth Salinger, she had etched on her back, sloping from her left shoulder towards her waist, an exquisitely executed dragonfly tattoo. Piercings in each nostril were homes for gold rings and completed the picture.

I don't suppose I shall see her again. She didn't look Hobartian. When she alighted and began to walk awa,y I peered through the window to view her feet. Footwear says a lot about the wearer. Sometimes shoes can be defiant, and I wanted to know what the message was in this case.

What I saw were soft hand-made ones, unsurprisingly unique. The picture was complete and I was left to wonder about this particular life. Another mystery that will never be unravelled.

The Cat Lady – another encounter: 2014

It's been some time since I've met the Cat Lady at the bus stop, so when we encountered each other yesterday, she asked me why. Had I not been going out? I gave her the reason, which is that I've been travelling earlier or later than the usual ten-thirty bus.

We sat together and I heard about her badly behaved young grandsons and her method of dealing with them; different, it appears, from that of the parents. That sounded to me like a very old story.

The Cat Lady, whose name, I am ashamed to say, I've forgotten, was sporting a mane of very fair, thick wavy hair and the sight astonished me.

At my previous meeting with her, she'd had it drastically cropped. This was due to recent neuro-surgery. She'd been prone to bouts of unconsciousness which would occur at any time and in any place. Before her operation, she'd advised me to turn her on her left side should she experience one of these alarming episodes while sitting next to me. I shall be eternally grateful that this never happened and I'm glad to say that she seems to be cured.

After we'd caught up with any items of news we deemed fit to share, the conversation turned, as it inevitably did, to the subject of her cats. A divorcee, living alone, they are central to her life.

She told me that she was grieving because she'd had one of her three precious pets put down. This cat had been suffering greatly from various ailments, including a constantly ulcerated mouth. 'I've been grieving for three weeks now,' she said, 'but I'm beginning to feel better.'

Her son-in-law, she continued, visited her recently. He stood in her doorway, his arms crossed, and appeared to be scratching his elbows.

She thought he must have had some irritating skin condition and asked him what was the matter. He entered her little villa, uncrossed his arms and released a small kitten; a female, as it happened. Her two remaining cats were doctored males.

She received the kitten with mixed feelings because, much as she loves felines, she wasn't relishing going through the training ritual. It was a bit like presenting a grandmother with a new baby. In addition, she would have the desexing expense and she'd already been charged a considerable amount for the planned demise of her old cat. She was, she confided, paying the fee by instalments.

The newcomer was not received kindly by the toms but was eventually accepted and is now part of the family. Apparently she sleeps between the two and her grooming is shared. The first cat licks one side, she turns over and the second continues her grooming.

After the Cat Lady's account of the death in her family, she told me excitedly that she was going to Africa with a friend. I thought this was to be in the very near future.

'No,' she said, she and her friend, who was born in Africa, are saving up and will make the journey in about a year's time. They are backpacking. 'I'm really looking forward to going on safari,' she said, and repeated, 'I'm so excited.'

When my Cat Lady is looking at the bigger furrier members of the cat family, I wonder how her domestic cats will fare: those who bid her farewell when she leaves the house and sit on her windowsill waiting for her to return; who even share her bed. Where will they go and who will cosset and love them as much as the Cat Lady does?

Commuting in Company: 2016

How many strangers did you speak to today? I mean *really* speak to, have a conversation with.

I plead guilty to the charge of pointing out too often the advantages of travelling by bus instead of by car. I like the words of Robert Bly in his poem 'Driving toward the Lac Qui Parle River' as he refers to 'the small world of the car, 'this solitude covered with iron'. So many opportunities to engage with fellow human beings are lost when one travels by car, necessary though that mode of transport sometimes is.

Yesterday I listened to mini life stories from two women.

I was waiting in Sandy Bay for the Taroona bus when an attractive woman of Malaysian appearance sat beside me – or, rather, placed her pile of shopping bags beside mine.

After a while, she said, 'Would you mind my parcels while I pop into this shop for a moment?' The shop was an Asian takeaway.

'Of course,' I replied.

In a minute or two, she returned with a package in a brown paper bag. 'It's my tea,' she explained.

So our conversation began and I learnt where she lived, that she'd been in Tasmania for twenty years and, before that, in Singapore, where her husband worked.

I asked her whether she'd be enjoying a family Christmas. She replied that the family was scattered but she did have a daughter living nearby.

Finally, she agreed with me that it would be nice to arrive home, especially because she had a severe headache. With these words, she boarded her bus.

If I'd been travelling by car, she would have registered as a dot in an amorphous cloud or perhaps, for safety's sake, not have been noticed at all.

My bus eventually arrived and I managed to juggle my bags so that I could mount it. I chose to sit on the seat reserved for the disabled or elderly, free for once, as it is usually occupied by fearsomely large boys or girls from prestigious schools. Sad to relate, they seldom offer to budge.

At the first stop, a woman of middling years staggered in with both hands only just coping with multiple carriers. The only unoccupied seat would not allow her to accommodate her parcels so I offered to place them with mine. She accepted gratefully.

Her seat faced mine, so we were able to converse. Somehow – and I can't remember how – the dialogue veered towards the woman's personal life.

She had been married and I'm not quite sure whether she was widowed or divorced, but apparently she had met a new man and it had been – at least on her part – love at first sight.

She became teary-eyed as she made this confession. 'It happens, doesn't it?' she said. 'You just know.'

I agreed. It certainly can be so. She related that the relationship was only a few weeks old. 'But,' she said, 'my grandfather glimpsed the frilled petticoat of a girl coming down some stairs. He said, "That's the girl for me," and they were married a very few days later. The marriage lasted until death parted them.'

That was a very happy and romantic tale and I hoped that her new relationship would follow the same pattern. I wished her luck as I left the bus.

Two strangers added interest to my life. We'll probably never meet again. The warmth of the encounters would never have been felt if I had travelled in that 'solitude covered by iron'.

A Reduced Circle: 2017

One by one, my bus friends are disappearing. Death and infirmity are the snatchers. I am beginning to wonder who will be the next to vanish and realise that it may well be me. The thought does not cause me great concern, though I would like to hang on a little longer.

The younger friends are still around of course and I was relieved to see my Shoe Lady board the bus after some weeks of absence. She was dressed in purple and wore the customary flower, not in her hair, as is the case in warmer weather, but on her beret. On her magic phone, she showed me photographs of her three-year-old granddaughter who lives in England. She is as pretty and animated as her grandmother.

Yesterday, as I sat shivering in the bus shelter, I said, 'Good morning' to a youngish lady whom I had observed for a number of years.

She replied politely and resumed her reading. She is never without a book but I have never managed to discover the content. She is of the type which many would describe as arty, with black hair coifed like Phryne Fisher's. She was once rather Junoesque but has become slim and wears idiosyncratic clothes. A tall woman, she makes a striking figure. What shall I call her? 'The Reader' perhaps.

I took out my tiny volume, a Penguin classic featuring two essays of Henry David Thoreau, one on civil disobedience, the other on reading. The subjects are interesting and I thought I should struggle with the difficult text.

'What are you reading, if you don't mind my asking?' said the Reader.

I held up my book so that she could see the title.

'Wow!' she exclaimed.

I confessed that I was finding it hard going. The conversation ripened and we spoke of crime writers and of Dickens. I hope that we will have more discussion in the future.

The Exercise Man continues his travel by bus and it distresses me to see him looking hollow-eyed and haunted. Why did he leave one of those troubled mid-European countries? Why can't he return? I dare not ask. He is well educated – even knows his Shakespeare – and I feel sure that he comes from a prosperous background. He notices what I wear and is often complimentary. That is very cheering for an elderly lady.

The exquisite little lady with whom I often used to travel has disappeared from view but I understand from the hairdresser we share that she has what is known as a 'package', which allows her to stay in her own home and she now travels in her carer's car. I heard from our hairdresser that in September she will be ninety.

I must close on a cheerful note. The Cat Lady moved to the eastern shore some time ago. She was very ill and still having her 'turns'. No one seemed to know how she fared and I confess that I imagined she was dead. Lo and behold! When I boarded my usual mode of transport recently, there she was, hair thick and groomed, a smile on her healthily rounded face.

She was very much alive and told me she was quite content in her unit on the eastern shore. A year has passed and I haven't seen her since that happy encounter. I like to think that death or infirmity have passed her by; that she's still enjoying life, now spent in close proximity to her family and – *of course* – with her beloved cats.

A Ballet of Fingers: 2017

For twenty-five years, I've travelled on the bus from my suburb to the city. For a while, it was an occasional trip since my chauffeur, my late husband, used to drive me to my destination – sometimes rather too speedily, I have to say. Now I use the bus regularly. I enjoy the journey as, through the window, I take in the beauties of the river and the sky in their various moods.

More than anything I delight in meeting different people, often discovering that they are more interesting than I might have thought at first. Only as aspects of individuals' histories become known through conversation are amazing lives recalled, revealed. Acquaintance often ripens into friendship of a kind. As 'oldies' (and they outnumber the young) we are unlikely to feature in that book – author forgotten – *Tales of Mystery and Imagination*, but ah! the past.

There are commuters whose behaviour is a little odd, to say the least, and they, unsurprisingly, are not particularly communicative.

Only recently, I noticed a newcomer in our midst. I had sat beside her on the seat at Franklin Square bus stop and was astonished when she suddenly engaged her hands in what I can only call a ballet. They are beautiful hands, enviable; small, white, delicate, the fingers with shell-like well-manicured nails. They fluttered from one side to the other. The movements were exquisite. After the performance, the manual dancers came to rest quietly in her lap.

A week or so later, she boarded the bus again and sat on one of the seats running along the sides. There are two, facing each other. She sat quietly for a while, her face impassive, then, unexpectedly, she BARKED then laughed before subsiding into silence and stillness.

To the credit of the schoolgirls on the facing seats, they did not snigger or cast their eyes upwards. No doubt they were startled as I was.

At home, I began thinking about the strange behaviour I'd witnessed. Something clicked. 'Ah,' I thought, 'perhaps she has Tourette's Syndrome.' During my working life (my paid working life), I was involved in special education and had heard of this condition.

I heaved my medical book (it weighs a ton) from the bookshelf which is devoted to reference books, since I have no relationship with Dr Google. I found Tourette's Syndrome under Nervous System Disorders and my suspicion was confirmed. I quote: 'The rare genetic disorder can manifest itself in uncontrolled movements of the head, arms and legs and repetitive shouts, noises, grimaces and spoken obscenities'. Naturally nothing was said about the sometimes unusual beauty of the arm movements, I imagine they are not common.

Just a few days ago, the owner of the dancing fingers sat near me. She was very quiet and still. One hand was captured, as if intentionally, by the strap of her very expensive-looking handbag. Perhaps she was making an effort to control her wayward hands.

Whose daughter is she? Are their hearts broken by her condition which, my learned tome informs me, is lifelong? Her smart haircut, her shoes (I've seen them in the window) from Icon, a very upmarket shoe shop in Collins Street, she has inherited but are no compensation.

Yet I wish I had the words to describe the beauty, the delicacy and elegance of those dancing hands, the unique choreography.

A quarter of a century of bus travel again leaves me with more questions than answers about my fellow passengers.

The Handkerchief: 2018

Travelling by bus, I have every reason to bewail the demise of the handkerchief. I believe that the young in particular would not know what a handkerchief is – 'a square of cotton, linen, silk et cetera, usually carried in the pocket for wiping one's nose et cetera,' says my *Concise Oxford Dictionary*. I am not sure what the et cetera embraces but that can be left to the imagination.

This lack of handkerchiefs amongst the passengers on my bus has made me the unwilling witness to practices too disgusting for me to describe. The very recollection of them makes me feel quite ill. I do not wish my friends to be similarly affected. I do, however, suggest a gloved hand if travelling by bus or, for that matter, when touching doorhandles, handrails and the like.

I believe that the handkerchief was invented by Richard II and in a film of the Shakespearean play of that name, the Duchess of Gloucester hands John of Gaunt a large and beautiful one, too beautiful for its use, though used it was.

People – mostly women – of my vintage will remember the morning admonitions delivered by mothers to their school-going children, the most important of which was, 'I hope you have remembered your hanky.' This needed to be displayed as it was at school later, along with fingernails and shoes, the latter required to be polished.

Lacking a pocket, a child sometimes had the cloth square ignominiously pinned to the chest. The bloomer leg was also a useful depository for it and no one seemed bothered by the sight of a strangely located bulge which does not appear in any anatomical drawings.

Attracting the attention of the opposite sex is much easier today than it used to be. Technology has taken over the role of the dropped glove or handkerchief – dropped, that is, in close proximity to the admired one, who would pick it up and return it to its owner. With a little cunning, more than a mere 'Thank you' could ensue; a conversation, which could lead who knows where. Poor Desdemona did not know to what horrible end her dropped handkerchief (embroidered, we are informed, so beautifully with strawberries) would lead – strangulation by a husband who called himself an 'honourable' murderer.

During the Second World War, hankies, if I remember rightly, were hard to find, as were bedlinen and dress fabrics. Was it this shortage or was it economy which led to the old, soft sheets being cut into squares, hemmed and dyed pink for the wiping of the nose et cetera? It was not too long before the real hanky re-emerged and was a favourite small gift for birthdays and at Christmas time. Teachers, grandmothers and minor aunts and cousins were thus blessed with what seemed to be an inexhaustible supply.

One of life's small pleasures is to use, or to see someone else use, a beautifully laundered white, lace-trimmed handkerchief. Such a sight is probably a delight confined to the elderly. A tissue, white though it may be, does not afford the same visual pleasure.

When a very much loved cousin of mine died, her daughter sent me two of her unused handkerchiefs. One of them I have kept as my 'crying handkerchief' for possible use at funerals or weddings. It hasn't actually been used because, although tears have risen to my eyes, they have not fallen.

Rummaging in one of my admittedly untidy chest of drawers, I found a handkerchief which brought back memories from my time in the UK. I feel sad that I have lost contact with the protagonist of this little tale.

I was waiting for the train to Euston and was sitting on a seat at the Hemel Hempstead station revising the *Universal Phonetic Alphabet*, something I had to master for an examination as part of the Diploma for the teaching of the Deaf and Partially Hearing. Next to me was a woman of about my own age who was also studying something which looked amazingly like the U.P.A. I remarked upon this and she replied that she was studying Turkish! I discovered that she was married to a Turkish judge who was for some reason a political refugee. I also learned that she managed a very respectable marriage bureau, the name of which I have forgotten.

We often met at the station and formed a bond. My husband and I dined with her and her charming husband and they with us. When we left England, she gave me the handkerchief, the lovely edging of which was worked by her mother-in-law. I have kept it ever since and regret that somehow I have lost touch with the donor.

It would be nice to see the resurrection of the handkerchief in all its elegance.

A Statement of Fact: 2019

My use of public transport is – sadly – fast diminishing but the other day I did risk the· bus ride home since I was not burdened with parcels.

Finding, after scanning the faces of the few fellow travellers, that there was no familiar one, I sat down, prepared to enjoy water views and treesy (please don't tell me there's no such word, because now there is!) gardens and with time to reflect upon matters which have been demanding attention for some time.

However, these matters were again put aside, as a statement which was attached to the partition between driver and passengers caught my attention. It said, 'Kindness Matters'. This was such a change from the usual admonitions which remind us of the naughty world in which we live: do not smoke, do not consume food on the bus, no bullying and remember that there are hidden cameras and you are being invigilated.

I had every reason to agree with the statement, which so surprised me, since I've recently been the recipient of numerous acts of kindness.

Since stricken with a rather serious illness some time ago, I've become a rather wobbly aged person who uses a stick; also one who finds negotiating slopes quite challenging. The condition has improved. I'm no longer terrified and am now only nervous, still having to steel myself to tackle the offending inclines.

Many people sense my insecurity and, unasked, enquire whether I would like to take their arm while crossing the road. These offers are very often from the young, both male and female, frequently from Chinese youth.

In the city on windy days, I am truly terrified and have been known to ask for the strong arm of the burliest man close to me. It has been given without hesitation.

It is not wimpish to be so afraid of a high wind. Now that taxis are my frequent mode of travel, I listen to anecdotes which would make interesting reading should they be compiled. One underlines my dread of a high wind when I am necessarily in the city.

My driver told me that one wild day he was driving along when a little old lady was painfully crossing the road ahead of him. He watched in horror as the wind actually lifted her up before she slammed down onto the road. Bones were broken and she was hospitalised. I did not relish the idea of such a fate, having no doubts at all about the verity of the tale.

Try as I do to be independent, there are times when I have to accept the accompaniments of senility, one being physical weakness.

The other day I decided to buy one or two items in Woolworths. I succumbed to the temptation of buying more than I intended (all necessary of course) and staggered out poorer, and laden with two far too heavy bags.

I had decided to bus home – not a wise decision – and wondered how I was going to cross the road to the bus stop without falling down midway. Next to me on the kerb was a strong youngish man holding the hand of a little girl. Still, one hand was free, so I swallowed pride and summoned courage, asking whether he would mind carrying one of my bags while we crossed the road. 'Give me both,' he said, and in fact insisted on toting them to the bus stop.

These anecdotes are only a few of those in store but I am in danger of becoming tedious.

Sometimes, though, it is beneficial to be reminded that people are inherently good; that 'a good deed in a naughty world' makes an impact, gives someone a better, happier day or perhaps even changes a life. Kindness matters.

A Digital Misadventure: 2019

It's taxis these days rather than buses but today I thought I'd support the Metro on my homeward journey.

There was no one I know travelling on the bus so, instead of chatting, I was able to observe the passengers opposite me.

Some may say that I have an unnatural interest in shoes. I won't deny it and I did check the footwear of those facing me. I can't remark on the man's shoes because my attention was riveted on the open-toed sandals worn by the woman. I tried to make my interest discreet.

There was nothing remarkable about the sandals. They were black, clean and neat. However, the exposed left foot was minus one toe – the one which should have been next to the big one.

You may understand my interest and speculation. How did she lose it? Was it amputated for health reasons or was an accident responsible for its loss?

I thought the woman very brave to wear open-toed sandals. If I were in the same situation, what I suppose is my vanity would make me choose an enclosed sandal (if that's not an oxymoron). When this fellow traveller left the bus, I saw that she walked with a limp, so perhaps the loss of the digit was due to an accident.

Of course I'll never know her story.

Finis: 2019

It grieves me to have to admit that I have joined the group which I've previously derided. In short (of necessity) I now travel in taxis – cars – instead of buses.

I've found, of course, that taxis are also a rich source of stories and my regular taxi driver regales me with his accounts of a misspent youth. Well, isn't most youth a little misspent?

He drives a red taxi but that's all right. I remember an aunt warning me – perhaps with tongue in cheek – to beware of men who drive red cars and sport moustaches. My driver friend does not have such a menacing adornment on his upper lip, so I'm safe. Safe, anyway, since my great age protects me from seduction from any source.

The bus stories that I have written are remaining fragments of a larger body, much of which I've discarded along the way. They have vanished as have my metro friends: the Cat Lady, the Exercise Man, the Shoe Lady, the Reader, the Mystery Man, Brian – all gone.

However, as I was walking to the café, I was heartened to see, when I turned in response to the call of my name, a once fellow traveller whom I privately call the Naiad, since her name resembled that of a sea nymph.

We are united in that we are members of the Slit Nose Club. Membership of this club has increased. To qualify, one must have had a malignant cancer removed from the nose. Brian, Naiad, the Cat Lady and I have all been under the knife. The surgery has been so miraculous that the casual observer would never know.

I sometimes wonder, perhaps mistakenly, whether this is the latest fashion in operations. In my youth, almost mandatory, were tonsillectomies, appendectomies, then later, hysterectomies. Only one of these had immediate post-operative advantages. Tonsillectomies, mostly performed on the young, were followed by ice cream and jelly. Who wouldn't welcome the prospect of the scalpel with such an attractive post-operative promise?

The Naiad and I greeted each other joyfully. We laughed about our walking sticks. She has had hers for a long time but her worsened hobbling was due to the painful stubbing of a toe. It's a dangerous world for us elders.

Today, after joining a friend for afternoon tea at a café in the city, I decided to return to my suburb by bus. I was not burdened by parcels and the vehicle was a kneeling one.

There were no familiar faces but I enjoyed looking through the window. The day was dying but it was a beautiful death. The tiered clouds were pink, grey and gold. Leafless trees were limned against the sky, black and lacey.

This is Heaven, I thought, after a long journey.

A Disrupted Journey –
a tale told in dreadful doggerel

It started well, the trip to Strahan,
With friends I've known since adult's dawn.
The river trip was what we'd wished,
Fantastic scenery, food well dished.
The rail trip then to that drear town,
Heaven help us, it's Queenstown!

There we stayed the night in digs
Which smelt of air spray and stale cigs.
Glad we were to quit the premises
Hoping they would meet their nemesis.
We thought our coach was bound for Strahan
In just a few hours after dawn.

Alas! We were two hours too soon,
'Twas timed for two and not for noon.
Meantime we had to peregrinate
To Zeehan, to pick up a mate.
Could we then please beg a lift
To occupy the unwelcome rift?

Of course we could, so off we went
Before the driver could relent.
The journey gave us lots of pleasure,
The time we had no cause to measure,
But on the journey back to THAT town
We were rather rudely flagged down.

Dismayed, we heard there'd been a crash;
The road was closed, we'd have to dash
Right back to Zeehan and change road;
No use to be in groaning mode.
We went as fast as we were able
And now –– more substance for a fable.

A young girl whispered to our steerer
News which quite alarmed the hearer.
The nether door had opened wide
And someone's luggage flew outside.
The coach was stopped and cases checked,
Two had gone, were no doubt wrecked.

Whose should the other be? My friends', of course.
What scenario could be worse?
The bus turned round, all eyes were peeled,
But no luggage was revealed.
Time passed by, our hearts were torn,
But we must board that bus at Strahan.

This we did, though very late, grieving at our dreadful fate.
(My old red rucksack was secure,
'Twas my friends who must endure)
When home at last, they went to bed,
Though not to sleep, they next day said.

All was not lost, next morn the phone
Conveyed a message, 'Do not moan'
The folk who tailed our sorry bus
Saw the missiles; with no fuss
Retrieved and took them to the station;
This the welcome information.

The case quite shortly was restored
Though its condition was deplored,
Its shattered carcass was mere trash
But no one had to part with cash,
For I had cases old aplenty
No matter if a little denty.

So one was received with gratitude;
I smiled at the beatitude.
Their homeward journey proceeded well,
No shame at all at the carousel.

www.ingramcontent.com/pod-product-compliance
Lightning Source LLC
Chambersburg PA
CBHW030917080526
44589CB00010B/345